# DEDICATION

For my mom,
(My #1 fan)

*You let me be me.*

My name is Alison
but my mom calls me Ali.

One day, in the spring, Mommy and I were outside in the garden.

It was a sunny day.

When we were pulling weeds,
I looked up at her and asked,
*"Shoes off, Mommy? Shoes off?"*

"*Okay Ali,*" she said, and then she bent down to take off my rubber boots.

I could feel the soil underneath
my bare feet.

*"Ahh! It's squishy!"*

I twisted and turned in the squishy soil, and my feet got dirty, but it didn't bother me.

I was free!

One day, in the summer,
Mommy and I went to the beach.

It was a hot day.

When we stepped in the sand,
I looked up at her and asked,
*"Shoes off, Mommy? Shoes off?"*

*"Ok Ali,"* she said, and then she bent down to take off my sandals.

I could feel the sand underneath
my bare feet.

*"Ouch! It's hot!"*

I jumped up and down in the hot sand, but it didn't bother me.

I was free!

One day, in the fall,
Mommy and I went to the park.

It was a windy day.

When we stepped on the grass,
I looked up at her and asked,
*"Shoes off, Mommy? Shoes off?"*

*"Okay Ali,"* she said,
and then she bent down to
take off my tennis shoes.

I could feel the grass
underneath my bare feet.

*"Oh! It's wet!"*

I ran through the wet grass,
but it didn't bother me.

I was free!

One day, in the winter, Mommy and I went to see the ballet.

It was a chilly day.

When the lights went down,
I looked up at her and asked,
*"Shoes off, Mommy? Shoes off?"*

"*Okay Ali,*" she said, and then she bent down to take off my fancy shoes.

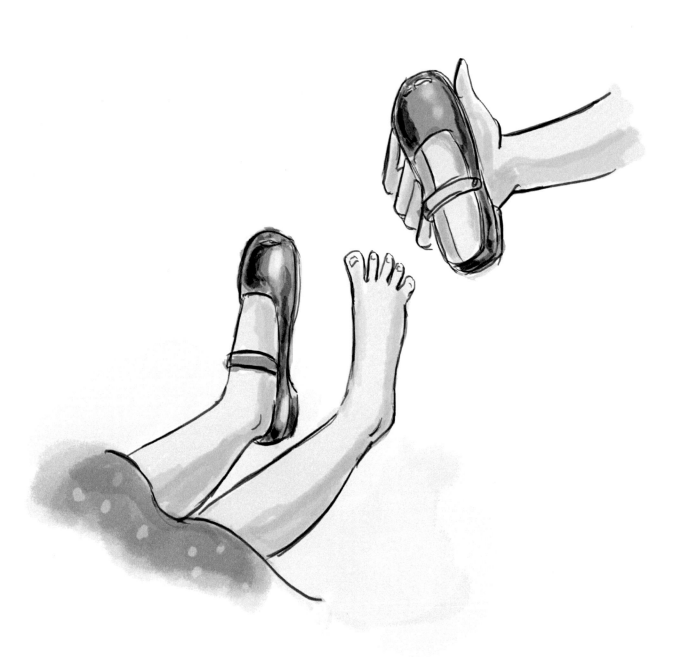

I could feel the concrete floor
underneath my bare feet.

*"Brrr! It's freezing!"*

I wiggled my toes on the cold floor,
but it didn't bother me.

I was free!

After the show, I told Mommy I wanted
to be a dancer when I grew up.

*"Okay Ali,"* she said, and then she bent
down to give me a kiss.

So Mommy took me to every
kind of dance class.

Tap class, jazz class, and ballet class.

I was happy,
but something didn't feel right.

Then one day, Mommy took me to a modern dance class.

The teacher said to the class,
"*Shoes off, everyone.*"

I looked up at Mommy with a big grin
and said, "*Shoes off, Mommy!*
*Shoes off!*"

I could feel the dance floor underneath my bare feet.

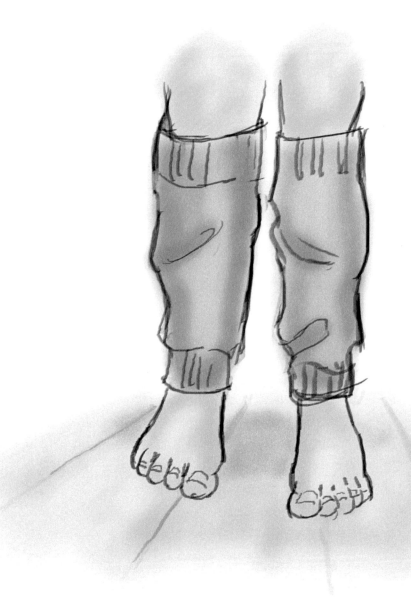

I twisted and turned.

I ran and jumped,

and wiggled my whole body.

My feet were sore,
but it didn't bother me.

I was free!

After weeks, months, and years of rehearsals, it's show time now.

Today is my big day!

I can feel the stage underneath my feet as I practice behind the curtain.

Suddenly, the stage manager shouts, *"Places everyone!"*

My heart begins to race and I am nervous.
But I take a deep breath and I remember
those times with my mom.

The curtain opens and the lights come up. I begin to dance, and although my feet are tired, it doesn't bother me.

Because never in my life have
I ever felt *so free!*

Made in the USA
San Bernardino, CA
10 September 2017